PERSISTENT

JEAN SHELDON

Persistent

Jean Sheldon

ISBN 13: 978-0-9838136-4-4

Library of Congress Control Number: 2015903164

Published by

Wellworth Publishing

www.wellworthpublishing.com
Oregon USA

To my dear friend
Mary Harding
(1943–2014)

Persistent

On countless occasions
during our friendship
I drew comfort and support
from a remarkable gift,
your compassionate ear.

Whether across the table
at a coffee shop,
or on the silent end of
a late night call,
you listened.

It was not your style
to give advice.
Instead, you offered
calm eyes,
soft nods,
and soothing sounds
should words intrude.

In one memorable exchange
you called me persistent.
Applied to the hesitant steps
and poorly marked paths
of my life,
the word surprised
and amused me.
But you had found,
as you often did,
a gentle way to call me on
my exuberant leanings.

Now, while you explore
vaster fields than this
earthly plane can hold,
I persist.

Safe journey my friend.
We will meet again.
Even the most persistent souls
let go when it's time to soar.

Contents

Electrical Storm

Clouds expand, scarcely aware
of the snow-covered peak
waiting to interrupt their flow.
But it would take an
entire range of mountains
to disrupt the mass of
crystals moving
across the sky.

I envy their journey,
sweeping past busy cities and
abandoned towns,
rolling over raging rivers and
sleepy streams,
floating above humanity,
unfettered and untamed.

I envy their journey,
and their ability to dissolve
as quickly as they form.

Mostly I envy those
fierce shows of emotion
that ignite the sky
on a hot summer night.

Crow Remembered

What is this solely
human need I have
to leave a mark,
to remind others
that I was here?
Will the day come
when I awaken
with no poems
to write,
no stories to tell?

Distracted by movement
outside the window
I see the black shape
of a crow watching me.
Has she heard
my thoughts?
Does she have
an answer?
Maybe, but she
doesn't stay for
conversation.

Instead, she lifts
her wings and
feathers spread,
vibrating the air
in a resplendent
hallelujah.

My busy mind settles,
humbled by the ease
with which she
leaves her mark.

Perfect Harmony

When unyielding night
cloaks you in doubt
and indifference,
cradle the hope of dawn.
It will come, and
when it does, let
the slow morning,
alive with promise,
comfort you.

And when the rush of
thoughts arrive, obsessed
with faults and failings,
make space,
but pay no mind.
What is peace if not
recognition of every voice,
whether discordant
or in perfect harmony?

Steady as She Goes

You were surprised
to lose your balance,
unsure if it was
the wind or a
societal shift that
pushed you off your
usually steady feet.

Remember,
you are human
and life
is change.

Loosen your grip.
Let the burdens
hold you steady
rather than
weigh you down.

You'll be amazed at
how like a feather

each perceived

problem becomes.

Then, whether the storm

is natural or manmade,

the choice will be yours

to hold tight

or fly.

Recipe for Success

An ounce of wisdom,
a touch of courage,
and the belief that
your savory offering
will nourish
a hungry heart.

Dialogue in a Church

A hinge creaks as I pull open the door.
I had meant my entrance to go unnoticed,
to carry out my research without the opinions
or advice of those with unquestioning faith,
to ask God directly about life and death,
and how to achieve them
in the proper order.

Embarrassed by my drab unholy attitudes,
I move to a dark corner, an empty pew,
where I kneel and rub my hands for warmth
and what might be seen as a prayerful pose.
"I seek answers," I tell God in a silent appeal.
"Don't we all?" (My thought, not God's.)

I question whether I am ready for this discussion
with a Holy Being, but remembering the
press of fear on my chest when squeezed into
a small space, unable to turn, barely believing
in a way out, I push on.

"Life," I suggest to the Creator of All Things,
"is not meant to be one long unhealed wound."

The church empties, candles flicker,
decades pass with no response.
One day I recognize my efforts to keep the
wound open. Slowly healing begins.

I had wanted instant answers from a god
of my creation,
to place blame, to define enemies, to assign
responsibility for every stumble, every fall.

With the unfailing support of others,
the salve of music, words, and art,
I discovered that life is not a wound, or a
collection of past and future struggles.
It is this breath, this kiss, this smile,
this song, this purr, this sigh. It is all that
we are, were, and will be in this moment,
and each day we grow more conscious
of that truth.

Looking for Peace

Looking back
the pain is sharper,
the blade thicker
and thrust with
greater force.

Looking ahead
the path is treacherous,
the climb steep,
and my shoes,
already worn,
begin to bleed.

"Close your eyes,"
the moment whispers,
"pay attention to me alone."

No pain, no blade,
no path to conquer.
This place,
this peace
is home.

On the Surface

Engaged in a conversation
that required exactly
the right word, I scoured
the beach for something
smooth and flat, an object
whose diameter allowed
my index finger to wrap
it securely, kept in place
with the tip of my thumb.
I released the treasure
side-armed into our
shimmering dialogue
and held my breath.
If calculations were correct,
the word would skip,
touching the surface
without breaking tension,
its reach measured
by ripples unfolding
at each gentle glance.

If the word were wrong,

or my delivery faulty,

it would hit the surface

with a hollow sound

and sink to the bottom,

dull and unheard.

I watch as circles expand,

and in a world of carefully

measured conversations,

savor the triumph of

my buoyant reply.

What We Expected

The spaceship Galileo
found Jupiter different
than we expected.
What did we expect?
What did we find?
What drives us
to understand the
farthest reaches
of our galaxy
and ignore
the universe within?
Keep the faith NASA.
And as we rise to each
new unexplored experience,
keep the faith humankind.

When It Rains

One day, without warning,
mud washed down the
mountain and covered my
life in thick grayness.
I had not given much
thought to the increasing
number of stormy days.
Nor had I realized that
minor events had a way
of accumulating until
even carefully constructed
walls could not
stop the flow.

Some good did come of
the unwelcomed mess.
I learned to pay attention
to even the slightest sprinkle,
and that carrying an umbrella
was not a sign of weakness.

One lesson took a bit
longer to soak in:
It is rain that brings the mud,
and rain that washes it away.

I Understood

At the sight of
my brother's body
returned home
from Vietnam,
I understood.
Form remained,
but light returned
to a timeless realm,
the infinite
before and
after.

When a week before
her death, my spirited
grandmother appeared
in a vision to invite
me across the
country for coffee,
I understood.
Those separations,
time, space, and distance

are illusions,
nothing more.

When even death's
barrier did not
silence your voice,
it took time,
but eventually,
I understood.
Only a belief in
solid ground
keeps me anchored,
and only a fear of
exploding into the
universe keeps these
expansive wings
pressed to my sides.

Mesa Morning

At another point on this journey,
inspired by the stark profile
of a sprawling mesa, I began
a ritual of morning prayers.

Not on my knees offering
repentance for debatable sins,
but parked on a rickety wooden porch
with a pack of lively dogs,
sipping coffee of a similar disposition.

I doubt the mesa noticed my presence.
Five years are not many to one
fifty million or so in the making.
But to this novice cowgirl, who
could not quite grasp beauty so large,
every sunrise made a new entry
in my soul.

Those high desert days are behind me,
and at times I struggle to separate memories
from dreams.

Do scrubby juniper still

pour long shadows

down the ragged slope,

or coyote, in fine voice, gather

for their nightly serenade?

I have yet to see a moon as large,

or stars as plentiful.

And nowhere have I found a

stillness so complete.

A reminder perhaps of

the silent unraveled universe

we shared

before this voyage began.

Old Words

I find

no comfort

in the

old words.

Even the

most clever

are heavy

with a struggle

to be

right.

So much

has lifted,

so much

will stay

behind.

Unobstructed View

When my limbs were as
strong and flexible
as the willow
in our backyard,
they carried me to
its highest branches
to scan the night sky
and survey the path
of my dreams.

The world spun at a
less frantic pace,
and my mind,
focused on rocky
footpaths and wild
new mornings,
gave no thought
to gathering years.

Today, limbs stiff
from climbing,

argue for fewer hours
folded in an office chair,
and eyes, parched by
robust suns, appeal
for views less harsh
than a computer screen.

While I have no doubt
that imagination is
best fueled by an
unobstructed view,
humor and wisdom,
the rewards of survival,
suggest the time has come
not to relinquish trees,
but to observe life
from branches a little
closer to the ground.

At That Moment

When you
have exhausted
every possibility,
you will lay
a gentle hand
on your heart
and remember
that you are
a part of
the whole.

A New Road

The path I followed ended abruptly and
left me with what seemed no choice
but to return to the beginning.
Not fond of wasting time or energy
I lingered amid a crowd of sturdy trees
and considered the constraints
of going forward.

There was my age, of course.
After six decades on trails designed
by others, was it foolhardy to attempt
to blaze my own?

Then there was the terrain.
What if just beyond my vision, obstacles
increased and brambles thickened into
impassable knots?

And surely, with so little sky visible above
the treetops, I had to consider the weather.

Was a storm brewing, preparing

at any moment to reenact a tempest

of biblical proportion?

As often happens in life—at least in mine—

the more I thought, the more reasons

I found to abandon my quest.

I was about to retreat when a small

forest creature dashed across my boots

into the ominous territory. The tiny hero

prompted an embarrassed laugh and

a sudden change in course.

With apologies to Mother Nature,

I stepped forward to forge

a long-overdue trail

of my own design.

Religion

I plunge into a nearly
frozen stream hoping
to remove ancient vines
grown tight around
my ankles, my thoughts.
They cling cold and wet,
filled with recriminations.
An old missal,
a discarded rosary.
A prayer, dredged from
sleeping brain cells,
reminds me that
"I am not worthy."

Religions teach self-loathing
and disconnect us from
the Source,
but a knowing guide waits within.
Listen, your heart knows
the way.

Encouraging Spring

If spring had need
of encouragement,
the ground might not thaw,
or crocuses wake
nodding velvet heads and
stretching verdant stems.

At times, though the outcome
is unclear, we are drawn
to take action,
to not wait for inspiration,
but to inspire.

With a trust of spring
in our hearts,
we abandon winter's grip,
open to grace and hope,
and prepare to take part
in the awakening.

Enough

We wandered the landscape,
food, land, and laughter
plentiful.

We settled in villages,
peaceful, united,
with bounty for all.

Armies invaded and
gave us their gods.
Friends became enemies,
there was never enough.

When an insatiable
need for power
destroyed us,
earth,
restored to all
but humanity,
was once again
enough.

From the Stars

I've often argued that
I am not a poet,
that I fill my messenger bag
with promises and guidance
gathered from the stars
and do my best to deliver
them unchanged.

But, if it is the job of a poet to
find inspiration in solitude
and share each point of light
revealed there,
perhaps I am a poet after all.

Getting It Right

We knew the miracles
were ours.
We knew, and
turned away.
Terrified to be gods,
we appointed others
to take charge.
One day we will
come to terms
with our godness
and create the world
we yearn for,
comforted by the
knowledge that
we are
bound
to get it
right.

Your Own Level

Water seeks its
own level.
Winding,
flowing,
unstopped by
massive boulders
or slender twigs,
moving as it has
for millennia
on familiar paths
in different forms,
here snow,
there rain.
A cloud that
greeted an
ancient civilization
returns to
renew a city street,
refresh a slender tree.

Remember, we are
largely water,
useful information
if life has pushed you
to your lowest level.

Ups and Downs

We look down to
measure our climb,
and climb because
to stay in one place
is against our nature.
Some fear a misstep,
a stumble,
a fall.
But those who
have learned
there is no up,
no down,
understand
the point has
always been
the journey.

The Things We Need

The sun tempts me from a desk
cluttered with loud chores demanding
attention to look out at my neighbor
weeding her garden.

Her simple effort to move plants
instead of paper fascinates me,
producing food we need to live
instead of snappy slogans persuading
others to buy things they don't.

At the end of the day,
soil stained and wrapped in the
scent of fresh air, she sleeps soundly,
while I stare at her garden,
pale, wide awake, and having
much less success stopping the
spread of invasive thoughts than
she had with dandelions.

Immeasurable Effect

Awareness brings compassion
and a softened heart,
a conscious state
reminding me
to make every action kind,
and every response one
of gratitude.

How Wise the Design

In a recent period of spiritual doubt
I sought refuge in nature,
a patch of grass that, while small,
was no less important than the
encircling galaxy.

Muting the chatter that ego brings
to every event, I sank into a lush
green carpet to consider the fear
that haunted me.

How wise the design that allowed me
to lie perfectly still beneath a giant
dome and witness endless change.

How clever the painter who countered
rich earth tones with soft pastels to
separate earth from sky.

How expansive the setting when the
brightest light departed to expose a
billion siblings dancing in celebration.

How rapid the conquest of fear
when both heart and mind opened
to fill with the stuff of stars.

The Connection

What about you is astonishing?
Your generosity, kindness,
your ability to forgive?
We are collectively
remarkable, you know.
When a powerful few,
hearts black with greed,
try to divide us,
to drive us to our knees,
we blink sleep-encrusted
eyes and take a stand.
Chins lift and hands reach
out to guide fallen sisters
and brothers to their feet.
We learn to talk beyond our
phones, to friend offline.
We like without icons
and share secrets without
counting characters.
The world moves forward,
global bonds grow,

joined by love

instead of hate.

Are we worthy

of this connection?

Oh, yes.

More than

we know.

The Next Step

I take a step and wonder
if it will define the worth
of previous journeys;
if every movement
forward or back
will be judged
by the direction
I choose now.

I whisper "Amen" and wonder
if this prayer will replace
earlier pleas for
guidance and grace,
or if past requests
for support apply to
coming storms.

I take a breath and wonder
if the arrangement of steps
and prayers really matters
in the scheme of things;

if, perhaps, what the
universe most treasures
are the steps we dance
and the prayers we sing
in any order we choose.

A Quick Recovery

Morning comes,
dissolving dreams
and shedding light
on the day's
first challenges.

I forgot to put
water in the
coffee maker.
A phone message
arrived in the
night with sad news
from a friend.

I consider crawling
back under the covers
to wait for a day
that welcomes me
filled with blessings.

Tap, tap, tap
from the paw
of a nearby cat
reminds me,
rather firmly,
that this morning
is exactly that.

Sweet Talk Me

Sweet talk me this morning sun.
Warm these wings still trembling
from the long dark flight.
Dissolve the fear that
feeds my anger
and when I awaken,
confused by the purpose
of this earthly form,
hold me in your
honey-sweet embrace
and assure me of
my place in the light.

Questions

Can you be sure the
ground is solid?
Or when the
sun returns,
will the weight
of a shadow
cave the earth
beneath your feet?

Are you certain the
boulder rolls downhill?
Or does someone
on the other side
push with equal
passion?

Are you confident
life is measured by
success and failure?
Or is the gauge
not the weight

of shadows
or the press
of gravity,
but the level
of love
in your heart?

Under the Bridge

There was so little
light under the bridge
that my body thought it
night and went to sleep.
Noise and traffic ignited
the surroundings,
but I slept.
Healing sunrises and
magical sunsets
propelled the world
on its rhythmic spin;
still I slept.
When a feral cat
joined me,
his body as
malnourished
as my spirit,
I went for food.

These are days of
plump cats and

a clear view of
rising and setting suns,
but I never pass a bridge
without checking for
those who might
be in need of
food or light.

Has Anything Changed?

I study the words of poets
whose voices, decades ago,
are as anguished as my own.
Has anything changed?

A baby cries from hunger and a
mother despairs at her failure
to find food.
Has anything changed?

Men threaten each other
in the name of their god,
in the name of their ego.
Has anything changed?

Voices join a global chant
proclaiming the "time is now."
To these urgent calls for change
I add my own.

Steady Stride

Footprints from days long gone
recall a path of survival.

Staggered first steps as I rose
from my knees.

Hints of strength in
a widening gait.

Then a strong steady stride,
a joyous return to the parade.

Perhaps it wasn't survival at all, but
a less common approach to life.
Can anyone look at their past and
find only perfectly spaced reminders
of where they have been?

A Cryptic Message

After days spent
knocking on the door
of an empty castle,
and nights filled with
a search for home,
I uncover a cryptic
message in my journal,
Spirit knows the way.
I don't know how
it came to be there,
or what it means,
but it makes me
wonder if Spirit is not
a powerful wizard
hiding in a castle,
and home no more
difficult to find
than a quick tap
of my heels.

On a Happier Note

We reached the finale
and the bassoon,
in complete despair,
let the story fade.
I teetered on the
edge of my seat,
living my own
tragedy,
not sure I could
bear to hear another.
Then a flute,
making a cautious
and youthful entrance,
brought a glimmer
of hope.
And though it seemed
an obvious play
for attention,
it lightened the mood
and set the tone
for a welcomed
happy ending.

The Mistake

At first only a whisper,
the slightest hint of
sadness,
but the feeling gains strength
bringing its own kind of
grief.
You know it too.
You've seen the color
drain from life,
but we never
discuss it for fear of
losing control.
The mistake I made,
for many years, was to
grab on and hold tight.
And isn't that the
biggest challenge,
letting go.

On Driving and Life

Slide the key into
the ignition and
depress the clutch,
give it a little gas,
turn the key and
move the stick
into gear.
Now, release the
clutch slowly and
be on your way.
Starting is easy,
but be prepared for
everyone
and their brother
to offer advice on
how to drive.

A Gardener and a Poet

For you
the night comes
too quickly.
Plants need moving,
ground needs cover.

For me
it is morning that arrives
too soon.
Stars tease the senses,
silence invites the muse.

Each in our way
we pray.
You kneel
to pat the earth.
I stretch
to tap the heavens.

Author Jean Sheldon

Jean Sheldon published her first book, *Jelly Side Down*, a collection of drawings and poems, in 1987. In 2015 she returned to the genre to release *Persistent*, another collection of poems, this time without the drawings. In the nearly thirty years between publishing her poems she has worked as a fine and graphic artist, published a number of mysteries, and found a great deal of delight in living each day to the fullest.

Made in the USA
Monee, IL
07 July 2026

56550172R00059